NEGRONI

DAVID T. SMITH & KELI RIVERS

NEGRONI

MORE THAN
30 CLASSIC AND
MODERN RECIPES
FOR ITALY'S ICONIC
COCKTAIL

PHOTOGRAPHY BY ALEX LUCK

RYLAND PETERS & SMALL
LONDON • NEW YORK

DEDICATIONS

Keli *For my mother who inspired me, my father who believed in me, my sister who put up with me and my brother who came after me. I love you all, especially after two Negronis.*

David *To Sarah Mitchell and Adam Smithson without whom the world of gin would not be what it is today.*

Senior Designers Megan Smith & Toni Kay
Head of Production Patricia Harrington
Editorial Director Julia Charles

Art Director Leslie Harrington
Publisher Cindy Richards
Drink Stylist Lorna Brash
Prop Stylist Luis Peral
Indexer Hilary Bird

First published in 2021 by
Ryland Peters & Small
20–21 Jockey's Fields
London WC1R 4BW
and
341 E 116th Street
New York, 10029
www.rylandpeters.com

10 9 8 7 6 5 4 3 2 1

Text © copyright David T. Smith and Keli Rivers 2021. Design and photography © copyright Ryland Peters & Small 2021

ISBN: 978-1-78879-279-0

A CIP record for this book is available from the British Library. US Library of Congress CIP data has been applied for.

Printed in China

CONTENTS

INTRODUCTION

When it comes to cocktails, there can be beauty in a simple recipe, but that is also where controversy lies: there is a wide array of arguments over the correct ratios to use and how to garnish a Martini or a Gin & Tonic. Another such cocktail is the Negroni. On the face of it, the Negroni is an equal parts mix of gin, vermouth and bitters (most typically Campari), but beneath that bright red surface lies a whole world of delights to explore and enjoy.

This book is designed to help you discover some of the joys of the Negroni from reasonably classic variations to the 21st century's White Negroni; these are followed by some variations using spirits other than gin in the experimental section and – finally – some seasonal treats, providing a Negroni for every occasion. Whilst the recipes often call for specific brands, these are just recommendations: all of the recipes have been designed to work with any classic London Dry Gin, including firm favourites like Gordon's or Tanqueray.

It is widely acknowledged that the Negroni was invented by bartender, Forsco Scarselli of Cafe Casoni in Florence, Italy in 1919 when regular 'Count' Camillo Negroni (the Count part has not been verified) wanted to fortify a popular drink of the time, Milano Torino (the beverage of Campari, sweet vermouth and soda that we now call the Americano). Scarselli substituted the soda water with gin and garnished it with an orange peel instead of the traditional lemon. The 'Count' himself was a man of many faces, moving to the Americas (to avoid the Italian draft) to become a cowboy, a banker in NYC and even a performing high stake's gambler in a Wild Wild West show. Like many classic cocktail origin tales there are a few contradicting stories – but what we do know is the first printed recipes of the Negroni, with three ingredients in equal portions, were published in 1955 in the UK and New York. However the drink was being enjoyed before then as Orson Welles wrote from Rome in 1947, 'The bitters are excellent for your liver, the gin is bad for you. They balance each other'.

The White Negroni is a modern take on the original that is growing in popularity; it was invented in 2001 by Wayne Collins for a French cocktail competition. As no Campari or red vermouth was available, he instead used Suze and Lillet. It wasn't long before his winning drink found its way to America via Simon Ford, then Brand Ambassador for Plymouth USA, and then to Audrey Saunders, of the Pegu Club in New York City. From there, as they say, 'the rest is history'...

The Negroni in all its incarnations has inspired social clubs, clothing, books, badges and pins; the cocktail even has a whole week dedicated to it in June! Such are the strong feelings of the drink's legions of supporters that some even have tattoos with slogans such as 'equal parts or die!' to show their dedication.

CLASSIC
NEGRONIS

NEWBIE NEGRONI

For many, the Negroni has the perfect combination of bitter and sweet complexity, but for drinkers coming across the cocktail for the first time, its intensity and bitterness can be overwhelming. This recipe has been designed to be a more gentle introduction.

The drink is both less sweet and less bitter thanks to the use of Sacred Rosehip Cup. This is made in London using both distillation and maceration of botanicals; including rhubarb, which adds a pleasant tartness. If Sacred Rosehip Cup is not available, try using a fruit cup such as Pimm's No. 1.

The drink will work with any dry gin or even, if you prefer, a fruitier style of gin. Moonshot Gin from That Boutique-y Gin Company uses botanicals that have been sent up into near-space on a weather balloon, so it makes not only a delicious drink, but an interesting talking point, too.

25 ml/1 oz. That Boutique-y Gin Company Moonshot Gin
25 ml/1 oz. Sacred Rosehip Cup (or Pimm's No. 1)
25 ml/1 oz. red vermouth, such as Martini Rosso
15 ml/½ oz. orange juice
25 ml/1 oz. soda water, or more to taste

GARNISH
lemon or lime peel
orange peel

SERVES 1

Add the ingredients to a large ice-filled wine glass and top up with chilled soda water. If the drink is still too strong, add more soda water. Garnish with lemon, lime and orange peels to serve.

THE CLASSIC

The drink that started it all – a perfect combination of three distinct ingredients in equal measures, that when mixed is better than the sum of its parts. Some people like to tinker with the proportions of gin, vermouth and Campari but to the authors this equal parts Negroni is sublime in its simplicity…

25 ml/1 oz. Beefeater Gin
25 ml/1 oz. red vermouth
25 ml/1 oz. Campari

GARNISH
orange twist

SERVES 1

Add the ingredients to an ice-filled rocks glass in the order they are listed here. Gently stir and garnish with an orange twist to serve.

Bar note Despite the strong flavours of the Campari and the vermouth, the choice of gin is really important and the Negroni is a great test for a gin's intensity and complexity. Beefeater is a classic choice with it's bright citrus notes; the legend that is James Bond prefers Gordon's Export as shown in the short story *Risico*.

BATCHED & BOTTLED NEGRONI

This is simply The Classic recipe in increased quantities, allowing you to make your Negronis in advance, which not only saves time (making one Negroni takes about as long as making a batched one) but also allows time for the ingredients to marry together in the bottle, giving the drink a more mellow, integrated character.

250 ml/10 oz. Beefeater Gin
250 ml/10 oz. red vermouth
250 ml/10 oz. Campari

GARNISH
orange twist (optional)

MAKES 10 SERVINGS

Pour the ingredients into a clean, 750-ml/25-oz. glass bottle using a funnel and secure the lid. Refrigeration is not essential but is recommended and gives the drink an extra chill. To serve, simply pour over ice and garnish.

Bar note This mix can also serve as a Negroni base for a number of other cocktails in this book.

BLENDED NEGRONI

There is something about 'frozen cocktails' – those that have been mixed in a blender – that is inherently great fun: they are simultaneously refreshing and somewhat reminiscent of childhood slushie drinks. Popular varieties include the Frozen Margarita or Daiquiri (strawberry or otherwise) and now the Negroni can join the party.

This drink needs a bold, flavoursome gin so that it still shines through after the blending. Golden Moon Gin, the creation of Stephen Gould, was inspired by a centuries' old recipe and comes from Golden in Colorado, USA. Tanqueray 10 Gin also works really well.

50 ml/2 oz. Golden Moon Gin
50 ml/2 oz. Aperol
50 ml/2 oz. rosé vermouth
60 ml/2½ oz. red/ruby
   grapefruit juice
6 dashes orange bitters
6 dashes saline solution
   or a pinch of salt

GARNISH
orange wheel

SERVES 2

Add the ingredients to a blender filled with ice cubes and blitz until the ice has broken into smaller pieces (typically about 30 seconds). Pour into Margarita glasses and garnish each one with an orange wheel to serve.

STOUT & STEADFAST

Whilst gin and beer may seem like an odd combination, it is well-rooted in the spirit's history. The Purl was a mix of gin, ale, sugar and spices dating from Shakespeare's time and a popular early morning drink for labourers, giving them fortification for the day.

20 ml/¾ oz. Boatyard Gin
20 ml/¾ oz. rosé vermouth
20 ml/¾ oz. St. George Spirits' Bruto Americano (or Campari)
60 ml/2 oz. Guinness (dark Irish stout)

GARNISH
orange slice

SERVES 1

Add the ingredients to an ice-filled half-pint glass and gently stir. Garnish with an orange slice to serve.

RUN FREE & NAKED

A slightly lighter drink, this recipe calls for cider instead of stout.

25 ml/1 oz. Conker Dorset Dry Gin
25 ml/1 oz. Campari
25 ml/1 oz. Punt e Mes (or other red vermouth)
300 ml/12 oz. dry sparkling (hard) cider

GARNISH
lime wheel or wedge

SERVES 1

Add the ingredients (except the cider) to a salt-rimmed, ice-filled pint glass and stir. Top up with chilled cider. Garnish with a lime wheel or wedge to serve.

DUNDORADO 1895

This drink could be considered the grandfather of the Negroni and dates from 1895, when it appeared in George Kappeler's book, *Modern American Drinks*. It is the earliest known recipe to combine gin, vermouth and bitters – the foundations of any Negroni. This is a modern adaptation of the original recipe.

25 ml/1 oz. Hernö Old Tom Gin
25 ml/1 oz. Antica Carpano (or other red vermouth)
25 ml/1 oz. Calisaya

SERVES 1

Add the ingredients to an ice-filled mixing glass and stir (the more you stir the softer this cocktail becomes). Strain into a cocktail glass and leave ungarnished as the original recipe did not call for one.

Bar Note Calisaya is a bitter liqueur originating from 17th century Italy flavoured with calisaya cinchona bark (red quinine), orange and other botanicals. It was discontinued some years ago, but has been resurrected by Elixr Inc. in Eugene, Oregon. An approximation of Calisaya can be created by mixing 2 parts Suze with 1 part Campari.

ULTIMATE PINK NEGRONI

The popularity of Pink Gin (the fruity, coloured varieties rather than the combination of gin and Angostura Bitters of old) has been booming in recent years. From strawberry to rhubarb, raspberry to hibiscus, these blush-hued products are here to stay and can make excellent Negronis.

   This drink uses Mermaid Pink from the Isle of Wight, which is made using surplus strawberries grown on the island and is less sweet than many of its contemporaries.

25 ml/1 oz. Mermaid Pink Gin
25 ml/1 oz. Aperol
25 ml/1 oz. rosé vermouth
   (such as Belsazar Rosé or
   Mancino Sakura is superb!)

GARNISH
strawberries and/or raspberries

SERVES 1

Add the ingredients to an ice-filled mixing glass and stir. Strain into a coupe glass. Garnish with strawberries and raspberries to serve.

SLOE-GRONI

Whilst most Negronis are made using dry gin, the full, fruity flavours of sloe gin, with its gentle sweetness, are a great companion for the herbal complexity of Campari. This is a rich and indulgent drink with a plump, jammy finish.

The London-based Sipsmith Distillery was founded in 2009 and makes fine examples of both dry and sloe gin, but any classic London Dry Gin will work in this recipe.

20 ml/¾ oz. **Sipsmith London Dry Gin**
20 ml/¾ oz. **Sipsmith Sloe Gin**
20 ml/¾ oz. **Campari**
20 ml/¾ oz. **red vermouth**

GARNISH
orange twist

SERVES 1

Add the ingredients to an ice-filled rocks glass and gently stir. Garnish with an orange twist to serve.

Bar Note Whilst the Sloe-groni and many other recipes typically call for Campari, there are a number of other bitters that will work just as well, such as St. George Spirits' Bruto Americano (which gives an added measure of earthy bitterness) and Tempus Fugit's Gran Classico (with its bright, bold floral citrus top notes) which are both well worth trying.

WHITE
NEGRONIS

WHITE NEGRONI

The white Negroni is typically less sweet than a red Negroni and has a strong, earthy bitterness with a light, almost marmalade, citrus lift to follow. The use of dry vermouth instead of Lillet makes the drink even dryer.

Plymouth was the original gin used when this drink was first created (see page 7) and remains a great option, but the gentle barrel-resting of the Hayman's Gently Rested Gin adds a pleasant mellowness and a touch of woody spice.

25 ml/1 oz. Hayman's Gently Rested Gin
25 ml/1 oz. Suze
25 ml/1 oz. Lillet Blanc

GARNISH
orange peel twist

SERVES 1

Add the ingredients to an ice-filled rocks glass and gently stir. Garnish with an orange twist to serve.

Bar Note Suze is a bittersweet aperitif from France that is bright yellow in colour and primarily flavoured with gentian root. Lillet Blanc is an aromatized wine from Bordeaux, which is flavoured with various citrus peels, as well as barks such as quinine.

CLARIFIED NEGRONI

A variation to impress the Negroni aficionado(s) in your life. This is a classic Negroni but with the characteristic red colour filtered out. It's challenging but well worth the effort to see the look on your guests' faces when you give them a colourless Negroni!

100 ml/3½ oz. Brighton
   Dry Gin
100 ml/3½ oz. red
   vermouth
100 ml/3½ oz. Campari
(or use 300 ml/10 oz.
   Batched & Bottled
   Negroni, see page 11)
20 ml/¾ oz. lemon juice
75 ml/2½ oz. whole milk

GARNISH
orange peel twist

SERVES 6

Make this the day before you intend to serve it.

Combine all the ingredients (except the milk) in a mixing glass and stir without ice. Add the milk to a separate, non-corrosive container and slowly add the contents of the mixing glass without stirring. Leave overnight (8–12 hours) in the fridge. The acid in the drink should cause the milk to curdle and this is perfectly normal.

Strain the liquid through a coffee filter or cheesecloth/ muslin to remove the curds before bottling the resulting straw-coloured mixture. Keep chilled in the fridge until you are ready to serve. To serve, pour a 50 ml/2 oz. measure of the mixture into an ice-filled tumbler and garnish with an orange twist to serve.

ULTRA-DRY NEGRONI

'Dry' is a term that's frequently used in the world of drinks, whether that be with regards to wine or gin. It typically means 'less sweet' and that's exactly what this drink is. It uses a dry fino sherry – the polar opposite of the rich, sticky dessert sherries that are often associated with Christmas.

25 ml/1 oz. Bombay Dry Gin
25 ml/1 oz. fino sherry
25 ml/1 oz. Cocchi Americano

GARNISH
grapefruit peel twist

SERVES 1

Add the ingredients to an ice-filled mixing glass and stir vigorously before straining into a chilled Nick & Nora or small wine glass. Garnish with a grapefruit twist to serve.

Bar Note Cocchi Americano is an Italian aperitif wine made with a base of Moscato d'Asti that is then fortified and flavoured with quinine (also used in tonic water), wormwood (used in vermouth and absinthe), citrus and other botanicals. It is crisp and citrusy with a slight, yet delicate, bitter finish.

GRAPEFRUIT NEGRONI

Grapefruits were once known as the 'forbidden fruit'. Originally from Bermuda, they only arrived in the US in 1823. This cocktail has been designed to complement the bright, zesty flavours of the fruit and the citrus oils notably round out the nose on the drink.

25 ml/1 oz. Cotswolds
   London Dry Gin
25 ml/1 oz. Aperol
25 ml/1 oz. rosé vermouth
15 ml/¹/₂ oz. white grapefruit
   juice

GARNISH
lemon peel strip
grapefruit peel strip

SERVES 1

Add the ingredients to an ice-filled cocktail shaker and shake vigorously. Fine-strain into a rocks glass (add more ice to the glass if liked). Garnish with lemon and grapefruit peels to serve.

Bar Note Aperol, like Campari, is a bitter aperitif from Italy. It is flavoured with a variety of botanicals including rhubarb, gentian and cinchona. It is most commonly drunk with prosecco and soda water in the popular Aperol Spritz.

KOKOMO

Here the Negroni meets the Mai Tai (usually a rum cocktail). This drink is fruity and fun with a light, creamy sweetness from the almond-flavoured orgeat syrup.

Portsmouth Fort Gin has been chosen as the recommended gin for this, as they make both a gin and a rum at their distillery, based in a Georgian coastal fort: Fort Cumberland.

30 ml/1 1/2 oz. Portsmouth
   Fort Gin
15 ml/1/2 oz. Suze
15 ml/1/2 oz. pineapple juice
10 ml/1/2 oz. lime juice
10 ml/1/2 oz. orgeat syrup
3 dashes orange bitters
pinch of salt

GARNISH
orange slice or wedge
fresh cherry

SERVES 1

Add the ingredients to an ice-filled cocktail shaker and shake vigorously. Strain into an ice-filled rocks glass and garnish with an orange wedge and a fresh cherry to serve.

NEGRONI BIANCO BERGAMOTTO

Italy is the home of the Negroni and this variation includes a few extra ingredients from the *bel paese*.

The Italicus Bergamotto liqueur not only comes in a bottle that is itself a work of art, but it is flavoured with botanicals such as yellow rose, gentian, chamomile and bergamot orange. The sparkling prosecco adds a bright zing and liveliness to this drink.

25 ml/³/₄ oz. Seven Hills Gin
(or Twisted Nose Gin)
25 ml/³/₄ oz. Suze
25 ml/³/₄ oz. Dolin Bianco
25 ml/³/₄ oz. Italicus Rosolio
di Bergamotto Liqueur
prosecco, to top up

GARNISH
orange wheel

SERVES 1

Add the ingredients (except the prosecco) to a large, ice-filled wine glass and gently stir. Top up with chilled prosecco and garnish with an orange wheel to serve.

Bar Note The peel of the bergamot orange used in Italicus Rosolio di Bergamotto Liqueur is most commonly associated with Earl Grey Tea and the gentian used is the key ingredient in Suze (see page 23).

WHITE ROSE

The white rose is a symbol of the UK county of Yorkshire, and, whilst any classic gin would work here, one from Yorkshire (such as Masons Yorkshire Gin, Cooper King Gin and Whittaker's Gin) is especially fitting.

25 ml/1 oz. Whittaker's London Dry Gin
25 ml/1 oz. white port
25 ml/1 oz. dry vermouth
3 dashes orange bitters

GARNISH
citrus rose (see method)

SERVES 1

To make a 'citrus rose' peel a long strip of lemon peel with a vegetable peeler and then roll into a circle, securing with a cocktail stick. Set aside.

Add the ingredients to an ice-filled mixing glass and stir vigorously. Strain into a chilled cocktail glass and garnish with the citrus rose to serve.

EXPERIMENTAL
NEGRONIS

AFTER-DINNER NEGRONI

This is a drink designed to be enjoyed after a meal, although you can, of course, drink it whenever a fitting occasion arises.

Whilst any dry gin would work in this drink, a slightly spice-forward one such as No. 209 from Pier 209 in San Francisco or Warner Edwards from Northamptonshire (UK) adds extra depth to the drink; in general, citrusy gins are recommended here.

25 ml/1 oz. No. 209 Gin
25 ml/1 oz. red vermouth
25 ml/1 oz. Campari
(or use 75 ml/3 oz.
   Batched & Bottled
   Negroni, see page 11)
25 ml/1 oz. freshly made
   espresso coffee, chilled

GARNISH
fresh cherries

SERVES 1

Add the ingredients to an ice-filled cocktail shaker and shake vigorously. Fine-strain into a cocktail glass and garnish with fresh cherries to serve.

BOULEVARDIER

This is perhaps the most well-known non-gin variation of the Negroni, described by drinks writer Paul Clark as, 'the Negroni's long-lost autumnal [fall] cousin'.

The drink is thought to have been invented by Erskine Gwynne, an American writer who lived in Paris and was a regular at Harry MacElhone's bar in that great city. The drink shared its name with the monthly magazine that Gwynne edited, 'The Boulevardier'.

25 ml/1 oz. Maker's Mark Bourbon
25 ml/1 oz. Cocchi Vermouth di Torino (or other red vermouth)
25 ml/1 oz. Campari

GARNISH
orange peel strip

SERVES 1

Add the ingredients to an ice-filled mixing glass and stir vigorously. Strain into a coupe glass and garnish with an orange peel strip, cut into the shape of a lightning bolt if liked.

Variation Try a Negroni Torbato, invented by Alessandro Palazzi of Duke's Bar in London – a smoky equal parts mix of Lagavulin, red vermouth and Campari.

OLD PAL

A lighter and less sweet version of The Boulevardier.

25 ml/1 oz. rye whiskey
25 ml/1 oz. Cocchi Americano (see page 27)
25 ml/1 oz. Campari

GARNISH
lemon peel spiral

SERVES 1

Add the ingredients to an ice-filled mixing glass and stir vigorously. Strain into a rocks glass (with ice if liked), and garnish with a lemon spiral.

MELA D'ALBA

Apple brandy, including the French variety Calvados, is not often used in cocktails, which is a shame as it can actually add a well-rounded, fruity and woody character. The Mela D'Alba (Dawn Apple) bucks that trend.

35 ml/1¼ oz. apple brandy, such as Calvados

25 ml/1 oz. Campari

25 ml/1 oz. Carpano Antica Formula (or other red vermouth)

GARNISH
lemon peel twist

SERVES 1

Add the ingredients to an ice-filled mixing glass and stir vigorously. Strain into a coupe glass and garnish with a lemon twist to serve.

Variation For a version that uses grape-based brandy, combine 25 ml/ 1 oz. Cognac, 25 ml/1 oz. Lillet Blanc, 15 ml/½ oz. Campari in an ice-filled cocktail shaker and shake vigorously before straining into a cocktail glass. Garnish with a cocktail cherry.

OAXACAN

Mezcal, the agave-based spirit from Mexico, is growing in popularity. It is often mixed with tonic water – a mixer normally associated with gin – but Mezcal also works particularly well in another gin drink: the Negroni.

25 ml/1 oz. Illegal Mezcal Blanco
25 ml/1 oz. red vermouth
25 ml/1 oz. Campari

GARNISH
lemon peel strip
lime peel strip

SERVES 1

Add the ingredients to an ice-filled mixing glass and stir vigorously. Strain into an ice-filled rocks glass and garnish with lemon and lime peels to serve.

BIANCO AMARGA

This interesting cocktail will appeal to fans of tequila.

35 ml/1^1/4 oz. tequila blanco
25 ml/1 oz. Suze
25 ml/1 oz. Dolin Bianco
15 ml/^{1}/2 oz. mezcal blanco

GARNISH
orange peel spiral

SERVES 1

Add the ingredients to an ice-filled mixing glass and stir vigorously. Strain into a sugar- or salt-rimmed coupe glass (as preferred) and garnish with an orange spiral to serve.

KINGSTON NEGRONI

This is a rum-based version of the Negroni that marries the herbal complexity of the cocktail with the warm, intense and gently sweet character of rum. It is named after the capital city of Jamaica, Kingston. The drink works with a variety of rums, but the best results come from using a Jamaican pot-still rum such as Smith & Cross, which is packed full of complex flavours.

25 ml/1 oz. Smith & Cross Jamaican Rum
25 ml/1 oz. red vermouth
25 ml/1 oz. Campari

GARNISH
flamed orange twist

SERVES 1

Add the ingredients to an ice-filled mixing glass and stir. Strain into an ice-filled rocks glass and finish and garnish with a flamed orange twist to serve.

Variation For a less intense drink, mix 25 ml/1 oz. cachaça (a Brazillian cane spirit) or white rum with 25 ml/1 oz. bianco vermouth, 15 ml/½ oz. Campari, and 15 ml/½ oz. lime juice. Shake in an ice-filled cocktail shaker and pour (without straining) the entire contents of the shaker into a rocks glass. Add more ice and garnish with a lime wedge.

KITCHEN SINK NEGRONI

This could be described as the Long Island Iced Tea of the Negroni world. It contains a variety of ingredients, each contributing to its flavour profile: the dry gin adds a botanical intensity, jenever adds rich cereal flavours, Campari adds its unique bittersweetness and the rosehip cup adds complexity. The vermouth then adds dry herbal notes along with the nuttiness of the sherry. Enjoy this drink slowly, and in moderation.

20 ml/³/₄ oz. St. George
   Spirits' Botanivore Dry Gin
20 ml/³/₄ oz. Bobby's
   Schiedam Jenever
15 ml/¹/₂ oz. Campari
15 ml/¹/₂ oz. Sacred Rosehip
   Cup (or Pimm's No. 1)
15 ml/¹/₂ oz. dry vermouth
15 ml/¹/₂ oz. Amontillado
   or Palo Cortado sherry
30–60 ml/1–2 oz. tonic water

GARNISH
lemon peel

SERVES 1

Combine the ingredients in a collins or highball glass and stir. Add ice and top up with chilled tonic water. Garnish with a generous lemon peel to serve.

TIKI NEGRONI

Picking up on the tiki trend, gin and rum are combined here to create a cocktail full of plump tropical notes with a balanced sweetness. The key to this recipe is the Plantation Pineapple Rum, a delicacy in Victorian England and the preferred drink of the Dickens' character Reverend Stiggins in 'The Pickwick Papers'. The pineapple has long been a symbol of hospitality; look at the lid on Tanqueray Gin and you'll see a pineapple.

Citadelle Gin is the creation of Alexandre Gabriel, also the man behind Plantation Pineapple Rum, and it is made in the Cognac region of France using no less than 19 botanicals.

25 ml/1 oz. Citadelle Gin
25 ml/1 oz. red vermouth
25 ml/1 oz. Campari
(or use 75 ml/3 oz. Batched
  & Bottled Negroni,
  see page 11)
25 ml/1 oz. Plantation
  Pineapple Rum
3–4 dashes Angostura Bitters

GARNISH
lime wheel
small pineapple wedge
pineapple leaves

SERVES 1

Add the ingredients to an ice-filled cocktail shaker and shake vigorously. Fine-strain into an ice-filled rocks glass and garnish with a lime wheel, lime, pineapple wedge and leaves to serve.

SEASONAL
NEGRONIS

IMPROVED SNOWGRONI

Advocaat is a liqueur made from sugar and eggs (much like eggnog) with a creamy, custard-like consistency. The festive Snowball cocktail is traditionally mixed with Advocaat and lemonade, with the latter adding a refreshing quality that balances out the liqueur's richness.

Here this hybrid of two classic cocktails – the retro Snowball and the perennial Negroni – balances the rich creaminess of Advocaat with the bittersweet intensity of a Negroni.

15 ml/^{1}/2 oz. Conker Dorset
   Dry Gin
15 ml/^{1}/2 oz. red vermouth
15 ml/^{1}/2 oz. Campari
(or use 45 ml/1^1/2 oz.
   Batched & Bottled
   Negroni, see page 11)
30 ml/1 oz. Advocaat
150 ml/5 oz. sparkling
   clear lemonade

GARNISH
lime wedge
cocktail cherry

SERVES 1

Add the gin, vermouth, Campari and Advocaat to an ice-filled highball glass and stir. Top up with chilled lemonade and garnish with a lime wedge and a cocktail cherry to serve.

CHOCOLATE LOVER'S NEGRONI

A drink for chocolate lovers on those special days, whether it be Valentine's Day, an anniversary or a birthday. A rich and romantic drink that makes an ideal alternative to dessert.

50ml/1¾ oz. Procera Dry Gin
50 ml/1¾ oz. red vermouth
50 ml/1¾ oz. Campari (or use 150 ml/5 oz. Batched & Bottled Negroni, see page 11)
40 ml/1¼ oz. crème de cacao
6–8 dashes chocolate bitters, to taste

GARNISH
grated dark chocolate
rose petals

SERVES 2

Add the ingredients to a cocktail shaker and shake vigorously with ice. Fine strain into two chilled cocktail glasses and garnish with a sprinkle of grated dark chocolate and rose petals.

Bar note Crème de cacao is a chocolate-flavoured liqueur and despite the name, it contains no dairy products. It comes in both white and brown varieties and whilst either will work for this cocktail, I do think the white looks better here.

Variation For a 'dry' drink, try replacing the crème de cacao with a dry chocolate spirit, such as Mozart's Dark Chocolate, which is full of chocolate flavour, but with less sugar than a liqueur.

SUNSHINE NEGRONI

The Negroni's answer to a Tequila Sunrise is just
as visually stunning.

25 ml/³/₄ oz. citrus-forward
   gin, such as Gordon's Sicilian
   Lemon Gin
25 ml/³/₄ oz. Aperol
25 ml/³/₄ oz. Dolin Bianco
10 ml/¹/₂ oz. orange juice
35 ml/1 oz. grapefruit soda
5 ml/¹/₄ oz. grenadine

GARNISH
orange slices

SERVES 1

Add the gin, Aperol, vermouth and
orange juice to an ice-filled highball
glass and gently stir. Top up with chilled
grapefruit soda and slowly pour the
grenadine down the inside of the glass.
Garnish with orange slices to serve.

Bar note Any grapefruit soda can
be used here, even something like Lilt,
but for the optimal visual effect it's best
to use a white grapefruit soda such as
Ting or San Pellegrino over a ruby or
red grapefruit variety.

PORCH-DRINKING NEGRONI

This laidback drink is made for sipping on summer evenings. The muddled strawberries give it a soft, fruity note whilst the bitter lemon adds a refreshing crispness. Plymouth is a widely available soft, sippable gin whereas St. George Terroir is intense and piney.

3 strawberries
15 ml/³/₄ oz. Plymouth or St. George Terroir Gin, as preferred
10 ml/³/₄ oz. Campari
10 ml/¹/₂ oz. bianco vermouth
150 ml/5 oz. bitter lemon

GARNISH
mint sprig

SERVES 1

Muddle (crush) the strawberries in the bottom of a rocks glass before adding the other ingredients and gently stirring. Add ice and garnish with a mint sprig to serve.

THE NEGRONI CUP

A longer version of the Porch-Drinking Negroni, this can be served by the jug/pitcher so is ideal for gatherings.

75 ml/2¹/₂ oz. gin
25 ml/1 oz. red vermouth
25 ml/1 oz. ginger wine
25 ml/1 oz. Campari
450 ml/15 oz. lemonade

GARNISH
lemon wheels
cucumber slices

SERVES 4

Combine the ingredients (except the lemonade) in a large jug/pitcher with ice and stir before garnishing with lemon wheels and cucumber slices. Top up with chilled lemonade and pour into ice-filled tumblers to serve.

RED HOT NEGRONI

Ice is an essential ingredient to a Negroni, but in the winter months that can be a bit chilly. This recipe turns a typically cool cocktail into a winter warmer.

There's a wide range of berry teas on the market today, but cranberry and raspberry works particularly well, and also gives the drink a suitably festive air.

25 ml/1 oz. Ableforth's Bathtub Gin
25 ml/1 oz. red vermouth
25 ml/1 oz. Campari
(or use 75 ml/3 oz. Batched & Bottled Negroni, see page 11)
125 ml/4 oz. freshly brewed red berry tea, hot

GARNISH
raspberries
orange wheel

SERVES 1

Add all the ingredients except the tea to a pre-heated latte glass (this keeps the drink hotter for longer) and stir. Top-up with the hot tea and stir again. Garnish with raspberries and orange peel.

Variation For a Red Bush Hot Negroni try mixing 25 ml/1 oz. London to Lima's Mulberry & Coca Gin Liqueur with 10 ml/ ½ oz. red vermouth, 10 ml/½ oz. Campari and 80 ml/3 oz. of freshly brewed hot Rooibos (red bush) tea. Pour into a teacup to serve.

NEGRONI ROYALE

A glamorous way to see in the New Year for those who find mere Champagne a little 'flat'. The Navy Gin brings some botanical power to help stand up against the other flavoursome ingredients, whilst the Campari and the vermouth add a balancing sweetness. Grapefruit bitters bring a lively zing to the mix, whilst the edible gold is one final, indulgent hint of decadence.

15 ml/^{1}/$_2$ oz. Hayman's Royal
   Dock Navy Gin
15 ml/^{1}/$_2$ oz. Campari
15 ml/^{1}/$_2$ oz. Martini Rosato
(or use 45 ml/1^1/$_2$ oz. Batched
   & Bottled Negroni, see
   page 11)
3 drops grapefruit bitters
sparkling white wine, to top up

GARNISH
edible gold flakes

SERVES 1

Add the gin, Campari, vermouth, bitters
and edible gold to a Champagne flute.
Top up with chilled sparkling wine.
This allows the flakes of gold to
dance up and down amongst
the drink's bubbles.
Serve at once.

NEGRONI FLOAT

A grown-up version of a drink that's been popular in ice cream parlours and soda fountains for decades. This surprising Negroni variation is indulgent, fun and delicious. The cola helps to lengthen the drink with additional botanical flavour and the creaminess of the ice cream complements the bittersweet flavour of the Campari.

15 ml/$\frac{1}{2}$ oz. **Campfire Navy Gin**
15 ml/$\frac{1}{2}$ oz. **Campari**
15 ml/$\frac{1}{2}$ oz. **red vermouth (or use 45 ml/1$\frac{1}{2}$ oz. Batched & Bottled Negroni, see page 11)**
1 scoop **vanilla ice cream**
100 ml/3 oz. **cola**

GARNISH
whipped cream
sprinkles
fresh cherry

SERVES 1

Half fill a large, tall glass with ice and add the gin, Campari, red vermouth and ice cream before carefully (and slowly) topping up with chilled cola.

Garnish with whipped cream, sprinkles and a fresh cherry. Serve with a straw.

Variation This recipe calls for classic vanilla ice cream, but you can have fun experimenting with different flavours; blood orange sorbet works rather well, too.

INDEX

ACKNOWLEDGEMENTS

The authors wish to thank:

The Gin Archive, The Gin
Genies, Nicholas Cook of
The Gin Guild, Gin Magazine,
J-money Barber, Charlie
Maxwell, Uncle Des, Bernie
Pamplin, Gin Miller, Emma
Stokes, Toby Gorn, Jules
Nourney, Aaron (AK) Knoll,
Alexandra Gerolami, Virginia
Miller, Queenie & Big T,
Clayton & Ali Hartley, Sarah
Mitchell, Adam Smithson,
Alessandro Palazzi, Kirsty
Loveday, The Hayman Family,
Eric Zandona, Bill Owens,
Wayne Collins, Benedict
Marston, Dan Szor, Dr. Anne
Brock, Stephen Gould,

Maritza Rocha-Alvarez,
Natasha Bahrami, Rosie The
Bear, Michael Vachon, David
W. Smith & JP Smith, Melissa
'Negroni Queen' Watson,
Rebecca Sturt, Jared Brown,
Lucy Ellis, JP Calabria, Rocky
Yeh, Zahra Bates, Mea Leech,
Sloane Kaplan, Jessica Maria,
Michael Valladares, Rocko
'Sugarbear' Valladares,
Summer Jane Bell, Janice
'Tiny Dancer' Bailon, Kimber
Weissert, Janice Snowden,
Claire Richards, Benjamin
Lawless Waterson, Robin
Nance, Christian Suzuki-
Orellana, Kellie Thorn,
Sarajane, Steph DiCamillo,
Siobhan Feeley, Allison
Webber, Kristå Kemple,
Diamond Ken, Sally &

Andrew Robinson, Michelle
& Jim Rivers, Muddy Rivers,
Kate Gerwin, Haley Forest,
Ben Peel, Magnus Tobler,
Juanjo 'John Joe' Maillo,
My Donkeys & their Burrito,
Leilani 'Elvis' Vella, Karri
Kiyuna, Michael Dekeyser.

We'd also like to thank Julia
Charles, along with Leslie
Harrington, Toni Kay, Megan
Smith and Patricia Harrington
at RPS who, once again have
been a treat to work with, and
thanks also go to Alex Luck,
Luis Peral and Lorna Brash for
creating the beautiful images.

Finally, a special thanks
to Sara Smith, without
whom the book would
not be possible.